Sa H.O.T.T.I.E.

Holy, Obedient, Teachable, True, Inspiring Excellence

Sanctify yourselves therefore, And be ye Holy, for I am the Lord your God! Lev. 20:7

Then I said I will not make mention of him, nor speak any more in his name. But his word was in mine heart as a burning fire shut up in my bones, Jer. 20:9a

Damita Jo Carthen

Sanctified and on Fire for God!
A Saved Sanctified Woman....

Determined to live for God
Devoted to ministry
Determined to be used by God
Loves the word of God
Determined to see God
A heart of praise
Determined to obtain the fruits of the Spirit
Free to worship
Determined to operate in the gifts of the Spirit
Slow to speak
Determined to pray, fast and study
Wears a smile
Determined to edify and uplift the body of Christ
Slow to wrath
Determined to help the needy, the poor and the elderly
Full of compassion
Devoted to her husband, family and children
Positive Attitude
Hardworking

Sanctified H.O.T.T.I.E.

All rights reserved. No part of this book may be reproduced or transmitted in any form or by any electronic or mechanical means, including photocopying, recording, or by any information storage and retrieval systems, without express permission in writing from the publisher, except by a reviewer's brief quotation in a printed review.

Copyright 2008, by Damita Jo Carthen

Library of Congress Control Number: 2008903044

Unless otherwise indicated, scriptures are marked from the Holy Bible, Full Life Study Bible King James Version, Copyright 1992 by Life Publishers International and/or The Message The Bible in Contemporary Language, Copyright 2002 by Eugene H. Peterson.

SANCTIFIED H.O.T.T.I.E. HOLY, OBEDIENT, TEACHABLE, TRUE, INSPIRING EXCELLENCE

Cover Design: Derrick Darks

All rights reserved. Printed in the United States of America

Sanctified H.O.T.T.I.E. is a registered trademark.

Dedication

This book is dedicated to my mother, Ms. Gwendolyn T. Bernard. Mom thank you for being my wall of protection, my wall to lean on, and the wall that kept me on the inside. Your example of strength and endurance has motivated me to grow stronger everyday. I am grateful for your friendship and guidance. Thank you for instilling in me a love for God and His word. Thank you for birthing in me how to be a lady and doing it with class! Class is birthed not learned, and oh how I know it now! I love you mom!

To my grandmother, Mrs. Anna Lucille Slaughter, the ultimate Sanctified H.O.T.T.I.E.! Your example of a devoted wife of 66 years, a mother of 5, a grandmother of 25 and a great-grandmother of 16, a sister, aunt, and friend will forever be a wonderful road map for many to follow. I love you granny! Your style, class and many shopping trips made me the classic shopper I am today!

To Mrs. Mary Vance-Williams, although I never got a chance to meet you, you are the true inspiration for this book. Thank you for birthing a son and instilling in him the vision of what a Sanctified woman should be! Can't wait to see you dance the streets of gold in your 4" stilettos!

Thank You

To God the Father, God the Son, and God the Holy Ghost, the head of my life, if I had ten thousand tongues I couldn't say thank you enough! The plan for my life is made perfect in you.

To all my children, thank you for allowing mom to be used by God. I appreciate you all. I love you with all my heart!

T-Baby, you have been my right hand, arm, leg and some times brain. I don't have words to express the level of appreciation I have for you. You're the best!

Andre' you have helped me be the woman that I am today, I am so grateful! You took the lead so many times as the man in my life. There are times when I have to stand in awe of your strength and wisdom. Most girls want there husband to be like their father… I want mine to be like you! I love you.

Dr. Kimberly Ventus-Darks, I do not have the words to express what your friendship means to me. From the first day we met over 25 years ago you have been the sister I needed. I love you!

Ruth & William Penn, sis & brother in law I love ya'll. Thank you for your encouragement. I am so glad that God believes in adoption--and then smears the blood line.

Sanctified H.O.T.T.I.E.

Dr. Darnell Thomas and Missionary Phyllis Thomas, of the Showers of Blessings Church, Sacramento, CA, your example of Godly leadership and your spirit of excellence have guided me throughout this process. You see I don't have to be there to remember your teachings. I miss you and love you.

Bishop Jeffery D. Thomas and my Mt. Rose Church family, thank you for embracing me as a sister.

Camille Travis, thank you for always being on the other end of the line! You will forever be my little sister, a true Sanctified H.O.T.T.I.E. I pray that God will continue to strengthen you and bless your every endeavor.

Carol Moore thank you for always telling me I can do it. I promise I will always be there …I understand you.

Derrick Darks, I have always admired your work, I am honored and blessed that I finally have a chance to work with you.

Michael Dailey, I didn't know how much I needed you until I needed you. Thank you for always calling it the way you see it. I will always appreciate your guidance and support.

Little Brother, your support of me has been tremendous! I don't know how to relay how much I love and appreciate you.

AND…to my friend, Leo Williams, who called me a Sanctified H.O.T.T.I.E., and started this!

Table of Contents

Dedication v
Thank You vii
Foreword xiii
From a Church Girl's Perspective xvii
Introduction xxi

Chapter One
    Sanctification, What Does it Mean to You? 1

Chapter Two
    What Does it Mean to be a H.O.T.T.I.E.? 11
        Holy 12
        Obedient 17
        Teachable 21
        True 26
        Inspiring Excellence 30

Chapter Three
    Who is? From Harlot to Heritage! 39

Chapter Four
    Are You? You Have the Tools! 47

Chapter Five
    Why You? Because You are Chosen for God's Purpose. 55

Chapter Six
    Be You! Promotion Comes From God! 63

Chapter Seven
    My Prayer for You 73
    What's next? 77

About The Author 79

Sanctified H.O.T.T.I.E.

Holy, Obedient, Teachable, True, Inspiring Excellence

Foreword

A Sanctified H.O.T.T.I.E. is a woman who is both envied by the world and the church for the exact same reason and at the exact same time. The world doesn't understand her and the church is often scared of her because of the innovative way God is using her in this new time. It is a woman who has it all! It is when you can be the finest woman in the room and filled with the Holy Ghost at the same time. A woman that walks with integrity, boldness and style but when you look closely she displays a deep level of wisdom and has mysteriously learned the art of holding back. A woman that the public may view as peculiar or strange because of her anointing but can't deny the fascination they have with her unique personality. Yes she has the unique package of being both sanctified and hot all wrapped up in one. The world envies her because of her style and sophistication and the church often doesn't understand her because of the modern twist on sanctification. Her holiness is shown through humbleness and her hot sass is found under her confidence. Yes she is both sanctified and very very hot!

See what the church doesn't quite understand is that it was Christ that made her both hot and sanctified. As a church we understand the sanctified part but we struggle deeply with the word hot! We have struggled from denomination to denomination with this whole notion that you can be saved and sexy, holy and sassy, sanctified and desirable!! We have struggled. The unspoken belief is that sanctification is girded in a dress to your knees, a

Sanctified H.O.T.T.I.E.

bland face with no make-up and hair tightly wrapped in a bun. But God is calling for women that can reach out to the modern woman of today and show her that she can keep her sass and still be saved. A desirable magnet to cross over to the other side and draw them in. We often confuse confidence with arrogance and sexiness with worldliness but if we stop being afraid of what we don't understand we would be more effective at winning souls!

The God I serve gives personality he does not take it away. He provides the confidence to wear bold colors, the "know how" to speak up instead of being passive and the sass to understand that despite your size or educational background that you are highly favored and that the world will bend at your presence. Yes, when you can know who you are, learn to walk boldly in it and then quickly give the credit back to Christ you become sanctified and with an anointing of hotness!

Finally… you have in your hands the book we have all been waiting for! A liberating, up scale and "on the mark" guide on how to live holy and still be sexy. What an "on time" book for both seasoned and young Christian women on how to absolutely be at the top of their game. How to live with sass from a secular perspective while still pleasing God from a spiritual perspective can be achieved. There is not a woman alive that will not be liberated and motivated by the book !!!

      Dr. Kimberly Ventus-Darks
      A.K.A
      "Dr. Kim"
      International Speaker, Author and Columnist

"We have struggled from denomination to denomination with this whole notion that you can be saved and sexy, holy and sassy, sanctified and desirable!!"

From a Church Girl's Perspective

I can clearly remember the first time I heard Damita say "Sis, I am writing a book and it is called Sanctified HOTTIE". Honestly I didn't really hear the word Sanctified, my focus was totally on HOTTIE. Please understand, I have been filled with the Holy Ghost for 43 years. That means I was 9 years old when I fully committed to serving the Lord. The church I attended was old time holiness and at one time watching TV was a sin. Sanctification was a process which usually ended up with you slain out on the floor. I participated regularly in tarrying services. For some who may not know, that is the act of praying until you receive the gift of tongues.

Although I have fallen many a times over these years I have always remained committed to serving God. And never once would I have thought of considering myself a HOTTIE. So needless to say, my initial thinking was you couldn't be Holy and be a HOTTIE. Absolutely no way, and anyone who thought so was just out there. Too far out there!

HOTTIE, the word alone conjures up and image that is an oxymoron to the word Sanctified. I sort of chuckled, honestly not thinking the book would materialize. As life would have it, the book is now available to you.

My initial attitude is why this book is so important. I began to think and consider the concept and asked myself

several questions. Does being sanctified mean that I have to be homely, solemn, completely covered and hidden? How can I attract attention to our heavenly father? What about me makes the world stop in their tracks and notice? When I contemplated the answers to those questions I instantly understood her perspective. As a woman of God we should not be average, we should be extraordinary. We shouldn't simply go quietly through life we should make a splash. The answers led me to realize when you truly commit to Christ; you qualify as a Sanctified HOTTIE. I chuckle again and count myself proud to be a Sanctified HOTTIE.

    Ruth N. Penn
    Evangelist/Missionary COGIC

"As a woman of God we should not be average, we should be extraordinary. We shouldn't simply go quietly through life we should make a splash."

Introduction

In an era of commercialism, can we find a virtuous woman, a woman of modesty, a woman of class, a woman of devotion and determination? While politicians and celebrities are setting the standard for women all over the world, is there a woman who will stand for Sanctification? A woman not afraid of her femininity while answering the call of God. Where is she?

Don't be fooled. This is not a trick question. Can one be Sanctified and still be a HOTTIE? Oh most definitely yes! Over the next few chapters you will read of some courageous woman each with a different beginning. At the end of their stories you will find them all Sanctified H.O.T.T.I.E.s.

What is a Sanctified H.O.T.T.I.E.? Is there a criterion? Will there be a background check? Who sets the example? Can you be a Sanctified H.O.T.T.I.E.? You may find yourself in the pages of this book.

Why write? When God opened the door and impressed upon me to write this book, I had to ask, "Who am I", 'Do I fit the mold of a Sanctified H.O.T.T.I.E.?" Is the description based on the external or internal woman?"

I was led to write during a period in my life when I felt truly alone. Talk about set apart! Having recently relocated from California to Texas, my life was being transformed. The move to Texas, newly divorced with six children in tow, promised definite change. Texas was a

whole new world, new church, and new friends! Old things are passed away, behold all things become new. I learned how to really talk to God about EVERYTHING! I thank God for the opportunity to get to know Him better.

While struggling to learn a new city, new schools and new people I had to deal with children who don't like change. Each of my children have different personalities. And oh boy did they not want to be in Texas. I found myself asking myself that very question. "Why am I in Texas?" Yes I began to talk to myself. Thank God for prayer. Most often when talking to myself the children thought I was praying---and sometimes I was. I was talking to God. The question kept forming on my lips and in my heart, "What now?", "Where are you?", "What do you want me to do here?" Saving grace came from finding a church home. After visiting and listening to confirming messages, I had been planted in the right place.

Having a determination to serve God completely helped me to stay focused. As I began to work in my new church home, my home began to fall in line. Don't get me wrong the devil had a plan. His plan was to continue to disrupt what God was trying to do. Through children with illnesses, ADHD, and just plain old defiance, I was un-detoured in my pursuit of God's face. My motto is: "Praise is Non-Negotiable". I will bless the Lord at all times; His praise shall continually be in my mouth! And I have learned and fully understand that if I acknowledge God in all my ways and trust Him, He shall direct my path.

Introduction

Always remember that our lives are predestined. Not just our spiritual life but our natural life as well. I continue to seek God daily for the plan for my life. I know that this book is part of that plan.

The term Sanctified H.O.T.T.I.E. was coined by a friend who referred to me in that manner. "Wow", I said, "What does that mean?" And here we are! What does it mean to be a Sanctified H.O.T.T.I.E.? Initially, Leo said, someone like his mother, Mary Vance-Williams, who he remembered shouting and aisle running filled with the Holy Ghost and doing it all in 4" stilettos! Mrs. Mary Vance-Williams who was devoted to her church, her husband and her children, never lost a shoe while giving God praise. To Leo, there was nothing like seeing a Godly woman, who displayed class and elegance, deliver the Word of God and/or shout in the Spirit! This was his vision of a Sanctified H.O.T.T.I.E. Several conversations later, we found that so many women could be considered Sanctified H.O.T.T.I.E.s. Women who may not shout or deliver the Word of God, but may be devoted wives, Sunday School Teachers, Youth Directors, the president of the Nurses Guild who never shouts, the woman who helps feed the poor, the woman who helps to find a cure for cancer, and so many more. We also ascertained that there is no age criterion, no height/weight requirements, no societal status requirements, no race or nationality restrictions or even religion boundaries. All you need to do is be able to answer these questions with YES!

Do you believe that Jesus is the son of God? And that He died, and that God raised Him up on the third day?

Sanctified H.O.T.T.I.E.

Have you received Him into your heart?
Have you repented of your sins?
Do you strive to live a life pleasing to God?

If you answered yes to all the questions, then a Sanctified H.O.T.T.I.E. you can be!

*"God's woman leads life!
She is not led by life."*

Chapter One

Sanctification, What Does it Mean to You?

"Set yourselves apart for a holy life. Live a holy life, because I am God, your God. Do what I tell you; live the way I tell you. I am the God who makes you holy". Lev. 20:7-8

To be set apart. To be set apart. To be set apart! How many times have you heard that?

Why is it that when you walk into some churches, the "sanctified" women are those in the front row, wearing "church" suits? Matching hat, matching shoes, matching stockings! Oh let us not forget the lap scarf/handkerchief with rhinestones and lace! Don't get me wrong some of these women are the epitome of a Sanctified H.O.T.T.I.E. They have paid their dues. They have been apart of the grand ole church all their lives, and have a true desire to live for God. They eat, drink and sleep the church and the word. These Sanctified H.O.T.T.I.E.s have formed a relationship and fellowship with God that gives them a sense of fulfillment, unwaveringness and confidence. It is displayed in the very way they walk, talk and carry themselves in and out of the house of God.

But who is to say that the young woman about midway back, with three children and no husband isn't sanctified? We do not classify her as sanctified because she doesn't wear glittery rhinestone studded suits with a matching hat and purse? Is it because we have never heard her say two words on a program? And just where is her husband? Do all those babies have the same daddy? Do these questions or the answers to the questions really matter?

We haven't visited her home. I say we should pay a visit. As we enter her home we sense a calm breeze gently touching our hearts. In her home we observe a devoted mother caring for her children in the best way that she can. She uses everything that she has learned to raise her children to be better than she. We see children who respect their mother even at play. In her we see determination. She is determined to see her children become productive and obedient members of society. She is determined that her children will love and respect God and His people. She is determined to be an example of a good mother. As an example she can teach her children the ways of Holiness. And when we look in her "closet" we may not find rhinestones and silk, but we find prayer. We find praise and worship, we find fasting and bible study. We find a woman of God, who loves God with all her heart and is determined to live a separated life for Christ. So while our sister may sit in the back of the church or mid-way back in a blouse and skirt she may be more sanctified than some of those who sit on the front row!

This young lady, if given opportunity for growth in ministry, will gain the self-confidence needed to walk with her head held high. She will learn that it is not what people think of her, it is what God knows of her. Learning and understanding that God is her life guide, she will begin to forgive herself for past mistakes. She will understand that each trial is just a stepping stone to get her closer to the prize. We will see new pep in her step. A swagger in her stroll. Sanctified H.O.T.T.I.E. she has arrived!

What is Sanctification? It is more than your clothes. It is more than how many times you are at the church during the week. It is more than being married and never divorcing. It is a determination to everyday set your heart on being different from the world.

Moving to Texas brought major change in my life. It took me from acquaintances, friends, family and loved ones and placed me where I knew no one but God. Guess what? That didn't make me sanctified, just lonely. My determination to continue to live a life pleasing to God, to live a life different from society has sustained me in my walk toward sanctification. The continuous redemptive work of the Holy Ghost is what aids me in my endeavor to be a Sanctified H.O.T.T.I.E.

Are you willing to turn your life over to God for the complete renewing of your spirit? Sanctification entails more than a simple moral improvement of character. Sanctification is the carrying on to perfection the work begun in regeneration, and it extends to the whole man

> *Neither yield ye your members as instruments of unrighteousness unto sin: but yield yourselves unto God, as those that are alive from the dead, and your members as instruments of righteousness unto God. Ro 6:13*
>
> *What? Know ye not that your body is the temple of the Holy Ghost which is in you, which ye have or God, and ye are not your own? 1Cor 6:19*

It is the special office of the Holy Spirit in the plan of redemption to carry on this work

> *And such were some of you: but ye are washed, but ye are sanctified, but ye are justified in the name of the Lord Jesus, and by the Spirit of our God. 1Co 6:11*
>
> *But we are bound to give thanks always to God for you, brethren beloved of the Lord, because God hath from the beginning chosen you to salvation through sanctification of the Spirit and belief of the truth: 2Th 2:13*

Faith is instrumental in securing sanctification, inasmuch as it (1) secures union to Christ

> *I am crucified with Christ: nevertheless I live; yet not I, but Christ liveth in me: and the life which I now live in the flesh I live by the faith of the Son of god, who loved me, and gave himself for me. Ga 2:20*

(2) Brings the believer into living contact with the truth, whereby he is led to yield obedience and embrace the promises of God for this life.

Being sanctified does not mean you have to be homely, unattractive, uninviting or even unpleasant. God's word says we are to adorn ourselves in modest apparel. I can not begin to count the many women, who live for Christ who are great models of Sanctified H.O.T.T.I.E.s, they are beautiful, desirable, gorgeous, sexy, classy, elegant and eloquent; Ty Adams, Cece Winans, Yolanda Adams, Maya Angelou, Vicki Yohe, Blanche McAllister-Dykes, Angella Christie and many more. And yet these same women dress modestly, they are humble, not overbearing, meek, loving and all the many attributes that God desires in a Sanctified H.O.T.T.I.E.

Being sanctified means the more holy you strive to be, the more humble, self-renouncing, and the more sensitive to every sin you become, and the more closely you cling to Christ. The moral imperfections which cling to you, you feel to be sins, and you try even harder to overcome them.

As you step into what God desires, you will see that you will become more attractive to Him and the world. When you are God's woman, you are the woman every man wants. There is an aura about you that man just can't put his finger on. People will begin to wonder why they are drawn to you. The word of the Lord says *"For the Lord taketh pleasure in his people; he will beautify the meek with salvation". Palms 149:4.* Salvation is your drawing card!

What does sanctification mean to you? Does it mean to be set apart? Or does it mean big hat, silk sequin suit, and a matching purse? Here is where you ask yourself a question. What is the battle? Is it sin or what you will wear to church next Sunday? Do you believe that because

you are at the church, doing church work every time the doors open, that you are sanctified? Do you battle with sin or with making sure you are in the front row at church? What is your priority being seen in the choir, on the praise team, at bible study, at every service or is your priority living a saved life? We must be careful of the battles we fight. Fight the flesh for it is your weak spot. *"Watch and pray, that ye enter not into temptation: the spirit indeed is willing, but the flesh is weak"*. Matt. 26:41

A Sanctified H.O.T.T.I.E. should of course find herself working. Whatever her hands find to do that is what she must do. While working for God it is ok to capture the attention of man, just make sure you direct man to God. Be aware of the calling and anointing God has trusted you with. Be careful not to take any credit for yourself. Your beauty, class, and elegance are all given by God. Make sure you use everything in the fight for salvation.

Remember it is not for us to judge if a person is sanctified or not. God is the righteous judge. He sees the heart. When God looks at your heart will He see a heart that is striving to set itself apart for a holy life? Will He find a woman who is doing what He says do? Living the way He says live? A woman trusting that He is God who makes her holy?

Perfect sanctification is not attainable in this life, we find this in Solomon's prayer of dedication; *"If they sin against thee (for there is no man that sinneth not,) and thou be angry with them…….. Kings 8:46"*. Solomon's words do not validate sin, rather, he expressed the truth that since sin is universally present, turning away from God is always a

possibility. We must strive to be in God's perfect will. In His perfect will we can come as close as possible while in human form to being truly set apart, sanctified.

"When you are God's woman, you are the woman every man wants."

Chapter Two

What Does it Mean to be a H.O.T.T.I.E.?

Holy, Obedient, Teachable, True, Inspiring Excellence

Hottie is a term used in the secular world for women who have a certain look. The secular stereo type of a hottie is normally of someone who is young, thin and extremely attractive; this may or may not be the case for a Sanctified H.O.T.T.I.E. In a by gone era, women typed as "hotties" were thought to be promiscuous, definitely not the case for a Sanctified H.O.T.T.I.E. Whether you are tall, short, skinny, fluffy, white, black, brown, red, yellow, blue, purple, short hair, long hair or no hair none of those things matter when it comes to being a Sanctified H.O.T.T.I.E. When you are a Sanctified H.OT.T.I.E, you are automatically cute, pretty, gorgeous, and beautiful.

If looks don't matter then what matters? Who you are and how you feel about yourself, is what matters! I am speaking to God's Woman, not the mother, not the wife, not the working mom, not the soccer mom, not the career woman. God's woman has a different perspective on the life she leads. That's right, God's woman leads life! She is

not led by life. She does not follow the road map that the world has given her. She takes the Word of God and blazes a trail for others to follow. She leads the way, not being held back by what the world says about her. The Word of God is her training guide. She makes a habit to study and continues her training daily. She steps out on faith and walks towards holiness.

Holy

> *Because it is written, Be ye holy; for I am holy. 1Pe 1:16*

> *For thou art an holy people unto the Lord thy God. The Lord thy God hath chosen thee to be a special people unto himself, above all people that are upon the face of the earth. Deut. 7:6*

A Sanctified H.O.T.T.I.E. is not flawless. She entered into a sinful world. She was born in sin; she strives to live a life free of sin. She may have faced sin up close, or contemplated sin, been in sin, but now her desire is to flee from the very appearance of sin.

Our very nature is a sinful one. A Sanctified H.O.T.T.T.I.E. must make holiness second nature. To make something second nature you must practice it. There are hundreds of opportunities everyday to practice holiness. In your office, at home, while driving in traffic, while grocery shopping, when hitting the Half Yearly Sale at Nordstrom's; you know all those things that bring others into our lives. These are the times when patience is truly a virtue. Can you practice, mercy, grace, long-suffering, patience, temperance when in an atmosphere of

chaos? Can you practice holiness in rush hour traffic and someone cuts you off? Can you make holiness second nature when, you have an unsaved boss, who tries your patience at every turn? Holiness, you must desire it whole heartily.

Holiness in the flesh can not be truly realized. True holiness will only be attained once we are changed in the day of the coming of our Lord Jesus the Christ. Why is that? Once we confess our sins we are Holy. We confess, we repent, and we are forgiven instantly and at that moment we are Holy. However, as I stated previously we are sinful by nature. David said, *"For I acknowledge my transgressions: and my sin is ever before me. Against thee, thee only have I sinned, and done this evil in thy sight; that thou mightest be justified when thou speakest, and clear when thou judgest. Behold, I was shapen in iniquity; and in sin did my mother conceive me."* Psalm 51: 3-5. It only takes one sinful thought to make us unholy yet again. God desires that we make every attempt to be Holy. This means we are to strive to walk in holiness.

> *"Wherefore, gird up the loins of your mind, be sober, and hope to the end for the grace that is to be brought unto you at the revelation of Jesus Christ; As obedient children, not fashioning yourselves according to the former lust in your ignorance; but as he which hath called you is holy, so be ye holy in all manner of conversation; Because it is written, Be ye holy; for I am holy"* I Peter 1 13 – 16

Why is it that people who attend church believe that they are better than everybody and that going to church gives them the right to treat people badly? Yes, that is general.

However, it is the statement that is made time and time again by people who do not attend church. I have encountered people who do not now, nor do they ever plan to attend church. Their reasons, "Because, I am treated better by my enemies on the street", they say. They also state that at least on the street they know where they stand with people. If someone doesn't like them or wants to cause them harm, they let them know it. Do you remember as a child, hearing that the fight would take place after school on the corner, or at the park? Both opponents were very aware of who was bringing the fight, the reason for the fight and where the fight would happen.

In our daily practice time, we should strive to kill the former lust. First we must understand that to lust does not just mean to yearn for sexual things. **Many times when we reminisce about our past we begin to desire that old life.** If you were a fighter in the past, whether by words or fist, there are times that if you have not girded your mind that first nature will show up and before you know it you are fighting again. Remember our first nature is a sinful one! When you come to yourself you have degraded, gossiped about, humiliated and treated your sister like she is not your sister. She went before the same court you did when she was adopted into the royal family. She is your sister! How can we say we love God whom we do not see and we can't even draw people to Him? Jesus said, through loving kindness have I drawn them. The same thing it takes to draw, takes to keep. Isn't that what we tell the men in our lives -- "the same thing it took to get me, it's going to take to keep me"

lol – the same principle applies to you as a Sanctified H.O.T.T.I.E. We are fashioned after the likeness of God, therefore our desire should be to be as much like Him as we can be.

Think about it. Would God do some of the stuff we do? Would God treat people the way we do? God is all powerful, all mighty, all knowing, yet He humbled Himself to walk along side of us. Sometimes we get a "title" and think it allows us to have special seating, which means "I don't have to sit next to "her" anymore", "She is beneath me", "and I don't even have to speak to "them" anymore." Please remember Sanctified H.O.T.T.I.E. you have NOT arrived! When you begin to feel that you are better than you sister, that is your first nature. KILL IT QUICK!

As I fore stated there are hundreds of opportunities to practice holiness. Our own flesh gives us the biggest run for our money. Gird your minds in the ways of God and you have won half the battle. Then bridle your tongue! I don't want to be known as ignorant do you? *"As obedient children, not fashioning yourselves according to the former lust in your ignorance; but as he which hath called you is holy, so be ye holy in all manner of conversation; Because it is written, Be ye holy; for I am holy."* Holiness has been given by Jesus Christ. If we trust Him, we will want to be like Him. We will pattern our lives after His. We will seek the gifts of the spirit that will continue to lead us into holiness.

Remember habits are formed during your daily routines. Bad habits are those mistakes that can be costly. Mistakes can cost more that you are willing to pay. Once you

decide you don't want to pay more than the cost of a gallon of gas for the lust of your flesh you will begin to perfect the good practices of holiness. You will walk daily with total confidence and maintain the highest level of moral character even in the most challenging circumstances. You will hold yourself accountable for the successes and failures.

We are in the fight of our lives. Our competition is fierce! Our competition is violent! Our competition is brutal! Our competition is vicious! Our competition is cunning! Our competition is bold and sneaky! Our competition is devious and ferocious! Our competition is cruel and malicious! Our competition is hurtful and just plain old mean!

Who is it? Who is our competition? Our first nature! Yes me and you, that sinful person that Jesus died to save. Strive to keep your competition out of the game! Never let your competition back in the game by allowing yourself to communicate at a level that is less than exceptional. The power of life and death is in the tongue.

Every time you utter a phrase within earshot of another human being are you speaking life? Truth is life? Truth flows from love. Love is God, and anyone who loveth is born of God and knoweth God. He who loveth not, knoweth not God. So how truthful are you? How well do you know God? Don't be caught ignorant!

Jesus shed His blood to bring salvation and continues to make intercession for us at the right hand of the Father. We should want that intercession to be light, not heavy.

Let's help to make His job a little easier, by walking in the things of God.

> *"A Sanctified H.O.T.T.I.E. is not flawless. She strives to live a life free of sin."*

Obedient

> *If ye be willing and obedient, ye shall eat the good of the land: Isa. 1: 19*

If someone asked you for the shirt off your back, would you give it? If you had just enough gas in your car to get home, but someone was stranded by the side of the road, would you give them a ride? Having nothing to feed your children and only enough money to buy dinner for the night, would you give to someone else in need? Operating logically, in self, in the flesh, you probably would answer NO to all those questions.

If God says clothes the poor and feed the hungry. If God says take care of the children. If God says take care of the widows. If God says go where I tell you to go. If God says say what I tell you to say. If God says be submissive to your husband. If God says honor your father and your mother. If God says obey those who have rule over you?

If Gods says all those things would you be obedient? Well would you?

To many of us obedience is a bad word? Because our flesh desires to have control, we find it hard to submit to leadership. Even God's! As post Women's Liberation Movement women we find it hard to submit to our husbands, or any other men for that matter. We are logical, and sometimes far too analytical. We must be able to see the outcome and/or the benefit of the sacrifice. Sacrifice? Yes that is what being obedient is about, sacrifice.

> *And the word of the LORD came unto him, saying, Arise, get thee to Zarephath, which belongeth to Zidon, and dwell there: behold, I have commanded a widow woman there to sustain thee. So he arose and went to Zarephath. And when he came to the gate of the city, behold, the widow woman was there gathering of sticks: and he called to her, and said, Fetch me, I pray thee, a little water in a vessel, that I may drink. And as she was going to fetch it, he called to her, and said, Bring me, I pray thee, a morsel of bread in thine hand. And she said, As the LORD thy God liveth, I have not a cake, but an handful of meal in a barrel, and a little oil in a cruse: and, behold, I am gathering two sticks, that I may go in and dress it for me and my son, that we may eat it, and die. And Elijah said unto her, Fear not; go and do as thou hast said: but make me thereof a little cake first, and bring it unto me, and after make for thee and for thy son. For thus saith the LORD God of Israel, The barrel of meal shall not waste, neither shall the cruse of oil fail, until the day that the LORD sendeth rain upon the earth. And she went and did according to the saying of Elijah: and she,*

and he, and her house, did eat many days. And the barrel of meal wasted not, neither did the cruse of oil fail, according to the word of the LORD, which he spake by Elijah. 1 Ki 17:8-16

This widow woman was the Sanctified H.O.T.T.I.E. of Zarephath. She was obedient not only to God but also to man. She sacrificed what she thought would be the last meal for her and her son to do what Elijah had instructed. Notice, however, flesh and logic spoke first, *"As the Lord thy God liveth, I have not cake......."* she pleaded her case. However, she became submissive as she listened to Elijah, the man of God, tell her what the Lord said for her to do.

How many times has a situation presented itself where God has wanted you to make a sacrifice? God has used people to tell you exactly what to do, but the analytical side of you argued your case and you didn't do it. God has spoken sometimes directly to our hearts, but we seem to talk louder than Him. Flesh says one thing, God says another who will you listen to? Flesh will fail you every time! Listen to God. Learn to be obedient to the spirit of the living God. God never fails!

Being a Sanctified H.O.T.T.I.E. means sacrifice. Women of the new millennium do not be so strong that you do not remember how to be a lady. Yes many women fought for us all to have the rights of a man. That fight was a good fight; fair wages, right to vote, medical and reproductive rights, the right to work in the same workplace as men and others. I am, as many of you are, happy for the fight. We are proud of the women who led the way for us to have the rights that we have now. We live better lives, can

provide for our families better and have a say in how we live in this country. It was a valiant fight! It was a tremendous victory for women everywhere.

However I say, we should still fight for the right to have our doors opened, our food orders placed at the finest restaurant, flowers delivered (just because) and our handkerchief picked up when we drop it! Never forget God desires for you to be a virtuous woman and your current husband or the husband searching for a "good thing" definitely wants to find a lady! Most men do not want a woman who can do everything he can do! Every man of God desires a lady of class, style, and elegance, full of virtue, love, femininity and God. Oh, did I leave out that the word of God instructs us to be submissive?

If the widow of Zarephath had not done as instructed she and her son would have surely eaten their last meal and died. However she was obedient and found herself with enough oil and meal for many days. When God asks for sacrifice it is not just so that He can be blessed but so that He can bless us. When praises go up…blessings come down!! When God makes a promise He delivers!!

Can you see how obedience is better than sacrifice? This widow would have sacrificed her life and the life of her child had she not obeyed the man of God. Trust God as she did and He will lead you into His perfect will.

Listen and judge not! What I mean by that is, sometimes God will speak to you and to you what He says or what He ask won't make sense. We do not know the mysteries of God. He knows the plans He has for us. Do not try to

dissect, or over analyze what God is saying. Just do it! Trust me it works! Well if you don't want to trust me, trust the Sanctified H.O.T.T.I.E. of Zarephath!

"Being a Sanctified H.O.T.T.I.E. means sacrifice."

Teachable

> *For the grace of God that bringeth salvation hath appeared to all men, Teaching us that, denying ungodliness and worldly lusts, we should live soberly, righteously, and godly, in this present world; Looking for that blessed hope, and the glorious appearing of the great God and our Saviour Jesus Christ; Tit 2:11-13*

At the age of 5 most children enter kindergarten, but years before that they are learning. It is said children begin to learn before birth.

Being born again means we have the opportunity to begin to learn at infancy. We are excited about learning. Do you remember when you first came into the knowledge of Christ? Some of you might have grown up in the church. Do you remember as an adult when you first realized God for yourself? All of a sudden He wasn't your mother's God or your grandmother's God anymore. He became your God. You wanted to learn as much as possible about this new savior in your life. If not careful anyone may have influenced you. But being in the right

church and submissive to leadership helped you stay grounded. You were like a sponge, soaking up everything you could about Jesus. You were at the height of being teachable.

Are you still that way? Or do you think you have arrived? A Sanctified H.O.T.T.I.E. remains teachable at all times. A Sanctified H.O.T.T.I.E. aspires to be excellent and she understands that to be excellent she most continue to learn. She recognizes there is always something to be learned.

To be teachable she remains open and submissive to the direction of the Holy Spirit and to leadership. No matter what title she may currently have, i.e., Missionary, Pastor, Evangelist, Minister, 1st Lady, Teacher or even President of the United States one should always be open to instruction. Through instruction wisdom is obtained;

> Get wisdom, get understanding: forget it not; neither decline from the words of my mouth. Forsake her not, and she shall preserve thee: love her, and she shall keep thee. Wisdom is the principal thing; therefore get wisdom: and with all thy getting get understanding. Exalt her, and she shall promote thee: she shall bring thee to honour, when thou dost embrace her. She shall give to thine head an ornament of grace: a crown of glory shall she deliver to thee. Hear, O my son, and receive my sayings; and the years of thy life shall be many. I have taught thee in the way of wisdom; I have led thee in right paths. When thou goest, thy steps shall not be straitened; and when thou runnest, thou shalt not stumble. Proverbs 4: 5-12

In verse 5 we are told, *"neither decline from the words of my mouth"*. A person is never too big to be instructed, your Pastor or Bible Study Teacher, should always find you attentive. This verse also says don't stay home when it is time to be taught.

Here we see a young lady who refused to go home. She had been taught about an Almighty God. She didn't want to miss out on what this "God" could do in her life. So Ruth stayed with her mother-in-law, Naomi, her teacher.

> *And Naomi had a kinsman of her husband's, a mighty man of wealth, of the family of Elimelech; and his name was Boaz. And Ruth the Moabitess said unto Naomi, Let me now go to the field, and glean ears of corn after him in whose sight I shall find grace. And she said unto her, Go, my daughter. And she went, and came, and gleaned in the field after the reapers: and her hap was to light on a part of the field belonging unto Boaz, who was of the kindred of Elimelech. And, behold, Boaz came from Bethlehem, and said unto the reapers, The LORD be with you. And they answered him, The LORD bless thee. Then said Boaz unto his servant that was set over the reapers, Whose damsel is this? And the servant that was set over the reapers answered and said, It is the Moabitish damsel that came back with Naomi out of the country of Moab: And she said, I pray you, let me glean and gather after the reapers among the sheaves: so she came, and hath continued even from the morning until now, that she tarried a little in the house. Then said Boaz unto Ruth, Hearest thou not, my daughter? Go not to glean in another field, neither go from hence, but abide here fast by my maidens: Let thine eyes be on the field that they do reap, and go thou after them: have I not charged the young men that they shall*

> not touch thee? and when thou art athirst, go unto the vessels, and drink of that which the young men have drawn. Then she fell on her face, and bowed herself to the ground, and said unto him, Why have I found grace in thine eyes, that thou shouldest take knowledge of me, seeing I am a stranger? And Boaz answered and said unto her, It hath fully been shewed me, all that thou hast done unto thy mother in law since the death of thine husband: and how thou hast left thy father and thy mother, and the land of thy nativity, and art come unto a people which thou knewest not heretofore. Ruth 2: 1-12

The story of Naomi and Ruth is a powerful one. There are many perspectives on why this particular story was written and why it is in the bible. Many people say it is a story of love, one of faith, one of obedience, a parallel story of redemption. I believe it is all of these and more. The continued instruction and learning that takes place in this book is something that should not go unnoticed.

Excellence is found in how she welcomed instruction. So many times we see, young ladies who take instruction as criticism. We must learn the difference between the two. How can you say that you are open for the Holy Ghost to instruct you, yet you will not listen to a saintly mother's instruction? Have you decided that you know who God will use and who He will not use?

I had the opportunity to be naive and un-teachable all at the same time. Being raised Baptist all my young life there was a noticeable difference when I joined the Church of God in Christ. Although I had been brought up "old school" Baptist, no pants in the church, not even in the

parking lot, and you had to "know" God before you could be baptized and take communion, there were some differences. Like the appropriate length of my skirts/dresses. I thought as long as I had on a dress or a skirt it was all good. At the time I joined the C.O.G.I.C. I was in my early twenties. You know, grown! And I had my suit skirts cut off and hemmed before they even left the store. In any event, each time I greeted the pastor's wife she would gently rub my leg and say "you have such pretty legs". Well having heard that all my life, there was nothing unusual about it to me. I took it as a compliment. Well one day while fellowshipping with some of the members I was asked if I had ever been told I need to wear longer skirts/dresses. "No", I replied, "As a matter of fact, 1st Lady thinks I have pretty legs", I proclaimed. One of the sisters asked me why I thought that and so I went on to explain to them what she said and did each time I greeted her. Everyone began to laugh. "Why are you all laughing", I asked. They then explained to me that was her way of telling me that my skirts/dresses were too short. I couldn't believe it. Why hadn't she just told me that? I know why. My demeanor then was "I am who I am and don't even try to change me". She knew that I would have taken her instruction as criticism. Guess what? I did. Even though she never said it, I began to stew over it. I thought to myself, "I pay for my clothes and no one is going to tell me how to wear them". "My mother doesn't even tell me how to wear my clothes!" I was so un-teachable. However, my mother had always taught me to never be a stumbling block. And the day that the Holy Ghost brought that to my remembrance, I lowered my hem.

Knowing that men are visual creatures and that all men are not as strong as they appear, it became my responsibility not to be the reason for weakness. Also, appearances can be harmful. Younger women or even older women could have taken my ability to wear shorter hems as ok to lower their standard. As we acquire knowledge it is up to us to cover others until they obtain the same knowledge.

Boaz not only instructed and covered Ruth in the fields but later in the story when she came to him on the threshing floor. If she had been seen leaving she would not have been able to get around the appearance of how it "looked". There are times when we need to be taught so that we do not appear to be ungodly. Take what you believe to be criticism is a new lesson to be learned and remain teachable.

That same type of instruction, guidance and covering is what we need to learn. Remaining humble enough to be teachable should be a goal for every Sanctified H.O.T.T.I.E.

"Being born again means we have the opportunity to begin to learn at infancy."

True

A true witness deliverith souls. Proverbs 14: 25a

> *Finally, brethren, whatsoever things are true, whatsoever things are honest, whatsoever things are just, whatsoever things are pure, whatsoever things are lovely, whatsoever things are of good report; if there be any virtue, and if there be any praise, think on these things. Php 4:8*

How many times have you heard "honesty is the best policy"? That term was coined by a natural man. True honesty is taught throughout the bible. It is one of the Ten Commandments "Thou shalt not bear false witness" that means you should not lie. A Sanctified H.O.T.T.I.E. should strive to be transparent. Transparency means you are clear, see-through. There shouldn't be anything that you need to hide. Oh I know many of you are saying "I don't want everybody to know my business". If you are about your fathers business what is there to hide? We are to show God in all that we do, if we are true, we can do this.

> *There cometh a woman of Samaria to draw water: Jesus saith unto her, Give me to drink. (For his disciples were gone away unto the city to buy meat) Then saith the woman of Samaria unto him, How is it that thou, being a Jew, askest drink of me, which am a woman of Samaria? for the Jews have no dealings with the Samaritans. Jesus answered and said unto her, If thou knewest the gift of God, and who it is that saith to thee, Give me to drink; thou wouldest have asked of him, and he would have given thee living water. The woman saith unto him, Sir, thou hast nothing to draw with, and the well is deep: from whence then hast thou that living water? Art thou greater than our father Jacob, which gave us the well, and drank thereof himself, and his children, and his cattle? Jesus answered*

and said unto her, Whosoever drinketh of this water shall thirst again: But whosoever drinketh of the water that I shall give him shall never thirst; but the water that I shall give him shall be in him a well of water springing up into everlasting life. The woman saith unto him, Sir, give me this water, that I thirst not, neither come hither to draw. Jesus saith unto her, Go, call thy husband, and come hither. The woman answered and said, I have no husband. Jesus said unto her, Thou hast well said, I have no husband: For thou hast had five husbands; and he whom thou now hast is not thy husband: in that saidst thou truly. The woman saith unto him, Sir, I perceive that thou art a prophet. Our fathers worshipped in this mountain; and ye say, that in Jerusalem is the place where men ought to worship. Jesus saith unto her, Woman, believe me, the hour cometh, when ye shall neither in this mountain, nor yet at Jerusalem, worship the Father. Ye worship ye know not what: we know what we worship: for salvation is of the Jews. But the hour cometh, and now is, when the true worshippers shall worship the Father in spirit and in truth: for the Father seeketh such to worship him.

The woman at the well is the Sanctified H.O.T.T.I.E. of Samaria! Yes the woman at the well with her torrid past and present. When she met Jesus she had several men, 5 to be exact and the one she was with at that present time was not her husband. She probably had gone to the well to draw water for him, the man who was waiting at home for her. When she met Jesus, He asked of her a drink of water, her response was that she couldn't believe a Jew asked of a Samarian, but it did not say she would or would not do as He asked. She was not aware of the sowing and reaping principle. That which you sow shall

return to you in abundance. She did not know that she had encountered the living water. What did He want from her? Was it just a drink of water? He desired truth and she was true in her response.

If Jesus were to ask you a question about your torrid past or present could you be truthful? What is in your past that you don't think He already knows? Our God knows all and sees all.

But the hour cometh, and now is, when the true worshippers shall worship the Father in spirit and in truth. For the Father seeketh such to worship him. I have heard over and over again my sister, Ruth, say she wants to be the woman that God is calling for in these last and evil days. I am sure many of you have heard those words time and time again through out your Christian walk. I hadn't heard it however until I joined the C.O.G.I.C. It sounds nice, as do all those other phrases that you hear people use during Testimony Service. How many people really know what it means? If I were to tell you that God is calling for you to be truthful in all your ways, could you do it?

Many times the fore mentioned scripture is used to say God wants pure worship. And I don't doubt that He does, however, this story of the woman at the well, tells of a woman who decided to tell the truth. Jesus went on to say that is what the Father wants; true worship. He does not want us to bring Him lies. You know the ones like; "O Lord I didn't know he was married, please forgive me", "O God I tried to say no to having sex with my boy friend again, I'm sorry", "Jesus you know I didn't plan to stay all night, help me", "Lord if you had made me a little bit

stronger I wouldn't have taken that drink", "Lord, I'm sorry for talking about the man of God" and let's not forget, "God help me to be a better person". We have a tendency to tell God what we think He wants to hear, when really He would rather us come clean. He wants us to be truthful about our lives; acknowledge our sins, and acknowledge our mistakes for what they are. We need to stop acting like He doesn't know who and what we are. We are sinners saved by grace.

If you want to be the woman that God is calling for in these last and evil days, you must tell the truth when you seek Him. The scripture says *"for the Father seeketh such to worship him."* If Adam and Eve could not hide what makes you think you can?

"If you are about your fathers business what is there to hide?"

Inspiring Excellence

Stir up the Gift

> *When I call to remembrance the unfeigned faith that is in thee, which dwelt first in thy grandmother Lois, and thy mother Eunice; and I am persuaded that in thee also. Wherefore I put thee in remembrance that thou stir up the gift of God, which is in thee by the putting on of my hands. II Timothy 2: 5-6*

The gift (Greek =Charisma) given to Timothy is compared to a fire that he must stir or fan into flames. The "gift" was probably a special gift and power from the Holy Spirit to fulfill his ministry. Note that the gifts and power bestowed on us by the Holy Spirit do not automatically remain strong and vital. They must be fueled by the grace of God, through our prayer, faith, obedience and diligence.

Paul writes to Timothy knowing that Timothy was timid and was facing hardship. Paul knew that Timothy was being persecuted from all sides, in and out of the church. Paul encourages Timothy to stir up the gift passed on by his mother and grandmother, Lois and Eunice. And to use said gift to guard the gospel, preach the Word, endure hardship and fulfill his charge.

Like Paul, I challenge you to "visit grandmomma's house more often". Go back find out and then pick up what grandmomma used to get her through. What did she use? It is that same Holy Ghost that gave her the strength to get through her trials and tribulations, that same faith in an un-seen God, that same obedience to the Word and leadership, that same determination to see what the end is going to be. Go visit the Sanctified H.O.T.T.I.E. of your earthly heritage, she will tell you that what it took for her, it is going to take for you; pray with out ceasing, singing "joy bells keep ringing in my soul" in the mist of a storm, overlooking the petty to see the big picture, diligent bible study, and honoring leadership.

Saintly mothers, and grandmothers, are the Sanctified H.O.T.T.I.E.s that continue to inspire us to be like them.

Just as Lois and Eunice passed a gift to Timothy, you have a gift that has been passed to you. Go visit grandmomma's kitchen listen to what she is humming. Can you hear a hymn? "Amazing Grace", "What a Friend We Have In Jesus", or "Rock of Ages", may be in the air, and as she cooks you can hear her talking to Jesus. Oh what a conversation. Yes, it is a conversation. He does have input because every once in a while grandmomma gets quiet and then shakes her head and says "YES LORD!" She is being instructed by the Almighty God Himself. We all need to visit grandmomma more often, if only in memory. What lessons can be learned from that Sanctified H.O.T.T.I.E. Our grandmothers encouraged and expected excellence in everything that they put their hands to.

My grandmother, when cooking a meal wanted everything, every time, to be perfect! I remember times when entire meals went into the garbage. If my grandfather gave the slightest look of not being satisfied, into the trash it went.

To this day my mother does not iron and the only reason I know how to iron is because I taught myself. My mother's distain for ironing came because my grandmother liked everything neatly pressed. EVERYTHING! Sheets, shirts, handkerchiefs, t-shirts and underwear, yes everything. And guess who had to do the ironing, my mother. I learned at an early age that there were cleaners who would launder sheets and package them and make them look like they had just been purchased. Although my mother didn't instruct me on the art of ironing sheets, she

instilled in me the desire to have things be neat, perfect, by pointing out those cleaners.

How many of us can remember going into our grandmothers drawers and finding things just right? The china cabinet was never dusty, the linen closet looked like the shelves in a department store, the kitchen cabinets were arranged for optimal convenience for cooking, and the spices just might have been in alpha order. Our grandmothers had a talent for making everything perfect. Excellence was their specialty. The way they set a table was perfection.

True Sanctified H.O.T.T.I.E.s down to the way they carried themselves in the home and out of the home. The way they could give you a look from the choir stand and no one knew what it meant but you. "Sit still and be quite", is what the look told me, and that is what I did. I cannot recall how young I was the first time I got that look, but if I got it now at 41 years old I would be obedient. That look stirred in me a need to behave, to be a good girl, to be "granny's good girl".

Granny's good girl, sat in church between other Sanctified H.O.T.T.I.E.s and acted like them, legs crossed at the ankle, hands folded in my lap, small handkerchief and tissues in my purse and my gloves in the cover of my bible. I remember at times thinking why do I have to sit with these "old ladies", I want to go with the kids. I am grateful today for the silent instruction of those "old ladies". The inspiration that was gained from watching the Sanctified H.O.T.T.I.E.s of that era is overwhelming. They inspired excellence in their every move, from the

way they stood, the way they sang the congregational hymn, to the way they turned the pages of their bibles. The way they responded to the preacher during the sermon was a true art form. Even the way they disagreed with something during the service was exceptional! Each of these ladies knew who they were and what they knew. Because of that knowledge they did not have to be boisterous or overbearing, they just simply made a note and slightly, ever so slightly shook their heads.

If you were to look up excellence in the dictionary it is defined as: the quality of being excellent; state of possessing good qualities in an eminent degree; exalted merit; superiority in virtue, the fact or state of excelling. Look the same word up in a thesaurus. Synonyms include: fineness, brilliance, superiority, distinction, quality and merit.

Notice that the synonyms did not include: perfect, flawless, unblemished or error free. No two people are exactly the same. You were pre-selected for the job God has for you. Your blemishes, your errors, your flaws are intended to help you learn and enhance your existing tools. They are also there to help you attain the cascade of benefits that come from practicing holiness.

Becoming a Sanctified H.O.T.T.I.E. who truly inspires excellence is not a Herculean task. In fact it is not a task at all. It is a journey. If you desire to please God you will find the journey rewarding.

What does it mean to excel? It means to go beyond or surpass in good qualities or commendable deeds. Keeping

the following scripture in mind, strive to walk in the light of God and you will excel. *"I saw that wisdom excelleth folly, as far as light excelleth darkness. The wise man's eyes are in his head; but the fool walketh in darkness"* Eccl 2: 13-14a

We all have the potential to be what God has called us to be -- Holy. Don't discount your potential.

"Go back and get what grandmomma used to get her through."

"Do Not Discount Your Potential to be Holy, Obedient, Teachable, True, Inspiring Excellence"

Chapter Three

Who is?
From Harlot to Heritage!

Likewise also was not Rahab the harlot justified by works, when she had received the messengers, and had sent them out another way? Jas 2:25

Can anyone be a Sanctified H.O.T.T.I.E.? Yes! There are many of us that believe that our past is too dirty for us ever to be considered sanctified. But our past is our training; our past has helped sharpen our tools. Whether you sold drugs or used drugs, God can use you! Whether you robbed, cheated or stole, God can use you! Whether you sold your body on the street or were involved in extra marital affairs, God can use you! God can use you, if you turn your life over to Him. *Therefore if any man be in Christ, he is a new creature: old things are passed away; behold all things are become new. 2Co 5:17*

As we learned in chapter one the redemptive work of the Holy Ghost aids us in becoming available for service. To reiterate, once a person takes the steps to salvation, you can achieve sanctification. We can achieve it by faith (Acts 26:18), by union with Christ (John 15: 4-10), by the blood of Jesus (1John 1: 7-9) and by the regenerating and sanctifying work of the Holy Ghost.

> *And Joshua the son of Nun sent out of Shittim two men to spy secretly saying, Go view the land, even Jericho. And they went, and came into an harlot's house, named Rahab, and lodged there. And it was told the king of Jericho, saying Behold, there came men in hither tonight of the children of Israel to search out the country. And the king of Jericho sent unto Rahab, saying Bring for the men that are come to thee, which are enter into thine house: for they be come to search out all the country. And the woman took the two men and hid them, and said thus, There came men unto me, but I wrist not whence they are:*

Rahab was a harlot, a prostitute, a sinful woman and of the Canaanite people who did not worship our God. However she abandoned her beliefs and came to recognize that our God is the only true and living God. Her past and present state did not stop her from using the tools she had at the time, a whore house, to aid Joshua's men. Her act was an act of faith, for she could not know that the men would save her and her family to be definite, but she had faith that the God of Israel could do it.

Her act of good-will and faith eventually secured her in the heritage of the Messiah. Remember no matter your past; if you come to Him and let Him use your tools you to can be member of the royal family with a rich heritage.

Some people let the past hold them hostage. It debilitates them. As a Sanctified H.O.T.T.I.E. you can not let your guard down. Do not let the past sneak up on you and make you a POW (prisoner of war). As women we have been hurt, used, mistreated, underestimated, demeaned,

and our hearts that we give so freely have been handed back to us, not just broken, but shattered.

Why? We have sought to fulfill the desires of the flesh. Fulfilling the lust of the flesh has left us feeling empty. To every woman who has had her own "whore house", trust me there are hundreds, millions more just like you. The difference between you and them is that you are now a Sanctified H.O.T.T.I.E. striving to live a separated life for Christ.

Coming into the knowledge of Christ hopefully you have learned that earthly man can never give you the affirmation you need, not by words, by deeds, or by flesh! We were designed to be mans help meet; man was designed to be the head, the provider, and the protector. We must understand as women of God that until he has a relationship and true fellowship with God the Father, God the Son and God the Holy Ghost he will not know how to love us. And the only man that can bring true affirmation is God.

Man's nature is a sinful one – back to chapter two. Man's desire is to fulfill the lust of the flesh. One look at a Sanctified H.O.T.T.I.E. and that is what he wants. Sisters we display what we are. Godliness is a drawing card, loving, nurturing, caring, encouraging, with the beauty given by sanctification through meekness. Your humble spirit and open heart speaks life. Your character and charm endear people to you. We must be careful that our God given assets are not abused.

Sanctified H.O.T.T.I.E.

All men have not come to understand that the anointing given to you to draw people to God can be misinterpreted. Men see and feel the anointing and that is what they want. That desire is manifested in a fleshly desire. That is why being a Sanctified H.O.T.T.I.E. is different than a secular hottie.

A Sanctified H.O.T.T.I.E. does not have to look a certain way to draw men. The anointing does it. A secular hottie has a fleshly appeal. You see because of the anointing man does not see what you really look like. Not to say that your natural beauty does not draw men to you, but the anointing of God has a supernatural appeal. Have you ever wondered why before Christ, you had to wear super mini skirts, low cut blouses and ultra tight jeans to get men to notice you? And then after the Holy Ghost got a hold of you, it brought conviction and modesty, now all of a sudden your ankle barely peeks out from under your skirts and every head turns as you enter the room. You are the same height and weight that you were before the anointing, what changed? You did! Man is still man, he is motivated by sight. However what he sees is now enhanced by God and boy does he want it. Unfortunately, like I said he has not come to understand the difference.

In his desire to fulfill the lust of the flesh he gets wrapped up in being with a woman of God and decides he needs to say all the right things. You know the things we need to here before we say "yes". And yes sisters we get fooled too. Because he is saying all the right things, and because he approached us in our new covered state of modesty, proclaiming his love for God, we think it's about a Godly

relationship. We then give into flesh. Somewhere between the long hem and the bedroom we lose sight of holiness. Is it a trick of the enemy? No. We are sinful by nature and we haven't had enough practice saying no to the flesh.

What do we do about this horrible mistake, this fall, this sin? Will God understand and forgive? Can we still be used? How can we learn from our failed test?

One thing about being a Sanctified H.O.T.T.I.E. is that it is a daily walk. It is being determined each morning to start over; each night repenting for the commission of sins, each morning asking for renewed strength, and seeking God for direction for that day. We press toward the mark – we have not arrived! As with Rahab, God has a plan for our lives if we are open to it. We learn from our mistakes and have faith that God will deliver us in our time of weakness, trials and tribulations. Trust me He will make a way of escape.

Do you think that Joshua ever imagined that his men would ever need the aid of a harlot? Do you think it was their intent to enter a whore house and be protected under its covering? God brought them out safely. Sanctified H.O.T.T.I.E. your act of faith will do the same for you. Your act of faith brings you directly into royalty!

"Sister's we display what we are."

Chapter Four

Are You?
You have the tools!

*And Moses said unto the children of Israel, See, the LORD hath called by name Bezaleel the son of Uri, the son of Hur, of the tribe of Judah; And he hath filled him with the spirit of God, in wisdom, in understanding, and in knowledge, and in all manner of workmanship; And to devise curious works, to work in gold, and in silver, and in brass, And in the cutting of stones, to set them, and in carving of wood, to make any manner of cunning work. And he hath put in his heart that he may teach, both he, and Aholiab, the son of Ahisamach, of the tribe of Dan. Them hath he filled with wisdom of heart, to work all manner of work, of the engraver, and of the cunning workman, and of the embroiderer, in blue, and in purple, in scarlet, and in fine linen, and of the weaver, even of them that do any work, and of those that devise cunning work.
Ex 35:30-35*

This chapter was partially inspired by a message preached by my pastor, Bishop Jeffery D. Thomas, entitled "Unpacking Your Bags". Bishop Thomas taught us that we are born pre-packed. Every tool that is needed to be of service to God was given to us prior to our birth. Our tools are authentic. Not everyone has the same set of tools. We learned that we cannot be anything we want to

Sanctified H.O.T.T.I.E.

be. But we can be what God has predestined us to be. Every assignment is determined by our tools.

When a person decides to become a carpenter, there are certain tools that he/she must purchase for that trade. If that same person decided to become a plumber they would have to acquire additional tools and there would be some carpentry tools that would go unused. If that same person then said no more manual labor I'm going into computers, the tools of that trade would be different. Each trade has tools designed just for it to aid in getting the job done. God has equipped us with tools for the trade He has predestined for us. He is actually equipping us daily for the task at hand. In other words He gives us daily what is needed to sustain us in our walk with Him. All we need to do is have faith.

Faith is a powerful tool. Faith in Jesus Christ is the only condition God requires for salvation. Faith is not only acknowledging Christ, but also an action coming from the heart of the believer to follow Christ as Lord and Savior.

The New Testament conception of faith includes four main elements: (a) Faith means firmly believing and trusting in the crucified and risen Christ as our personal Lord and Savior. It involves believing from our heart, which is yielding up our will and committing our total self to Jesus Christ as He is revealed in the New Testament. (b) Faith involves repentance, i.e., turning from sin with true regret and turning to God through Christ. (c) Faith includes obedience to Jesus Christ and His Word as a way of life inspired by our faith, by our gratitude to God, and by the regenerating work of the

Holy Spirit. Hence, faith and obedience belong inseparably together. (d) Faith includes a heartfelt personal devotion and attachment to Jesus Christ that expresses itself in trust, love, gratitude, and loyalty toward Him. Faith in an ultimate sense cannot properly be distinguished from love.

Faith in Jesus as Lord and Savior is both the act of a single moment and a continuing attitude for life that must grow.

A woman made an act, a single moment, which changed her life forever. I am sure if the story had continued she would testify years later that she still had faith in Jesus.

> *And a woman having an issue of blood twelve years, which had spent all her living upon physicians, neither could be healed of any, Came behind him, and touched the border of his garment: and immediately her issue of blood stanched. And Jesus said, Who touched me? When all denied, Peter and they that were with him said, Master, the multitude throng thee and press thee, and sayest thou, Who touched me? And Jesus said, Somebody hath touched me: for I perceive that virtue is gone out of me. And when the woman saw that she was not hid, she came trembling, and falling down before him, she declared unto him before all the people for what cause she had touched him, and how she was healed immediately. And he said unto her, Daughter, be of good comfort: thy faith hath made thee whole; go in peace. Luke 8: 43-48*

This woman had several authentic tools. A true Sanctified H.O.T.T.I.E. looks at everything that makes her a woman, as a tool. Believe it or not this woman's first tool was her illness. Yes, her illness! Her illness was the tool that

taught her endurance, patience, being slow to anger and despair, which is longsuffering. It was able to chisel out meekness, which is restraint coupled with strength and courage. And the giant tool created, quite possibly the first tool, was faith. Her faith carved out persistence. She had many tools, but such a short story. However, it took 12 years for the tools to form a woman who was persistent in her position.

Persistence in her position was what was needed by this woman. She was determined to get to Jesus. After twelve years of patience with doctors. Twelve years of enduring, pain and abandonment. Twelve years of despair from no cure. Twelve years of being angry, and restraining that anger. Twelve years of courage to continue to get up every morning and try something different. Twelve years of gaining strength in her trial. She was persistent. She would be made whole. She would be healed. And when she heard of a man who could give her the cure she needed she believed, had faith, that he could do it. Cure her. She had not seen Jesus, but she believed. She said, *"If I may touch but his clothes, I shall be whole"* Mark 5: 28. Although Jesus had a crowd of people around Him and surely several people were touching Him, this woman was persistent in her determination to get to Jesus. Her position was to touch but his garment by any means necessary. Her persistent through her trial brought her to Jesus. Her faith made her whole.

Are you persistent in your position? In the path of life there are many curves in the road, many hills to climb, several valleys to cross, mountains to go around and one

can encounter pot holes, several pot holes. A Sanctified H.O.T.T.I.E. must being willing to acknowledge that she can fall. Her persistent, however, tells her that when she falls she must get back up. Having an unyielding determination to be or to do something for God daily is being persistent in your position. Remember a Sanctified H.O.T.T.I.E.s position should be one of Holy, Obedient, Teachable, True and Inspiring Excellence.

"Are you persistent in your position?"

Chapter Five

Why You? Because you are chosen for God's purpose

And we know that all things work together to them that love God, to them who are the called according to his purpose.
Romans 8:28

Before you ever knew of a gracious, merciful, loving God, He was thinking about you. God is omnipresent, omniscient, and omnipotent! Through every problem, trial and tribulation He was there and is there.

You may now or at one time have felt like you were not worthy of God's love. Remember God created you in the likeness of Himself. At times we may get lost in believing that what we have done is so bad that we can never make it better. Jesus came so that we might have life and have it more abundantly. You can be a Sanctified H.O.T.T.I.E., even though at times you may not believe it.

There is a very special young lady in my life that I have seen glowing in God's light and I have seen the light from within dim. She has three wonderful children and she loves them dearly, but at one time she did not have the ability to raise them. Their father a convicted drug dealer

in jail, a marriage gone bad and some major church hurt took her from being a vibrant, hardworking young lady to the streets. Into the world she went in search of comfort, sympathy, and understanding. I was horrified to learn that she no longer was striving to live a life for Christ. She no longer had a job and no longer had her children. The only blessing I could see was her praying and faithful mother. Her mother stepped in to raise the children and continued to pray. My young friend remained out of fellowship with God in the world for 4 years while her mother, I and many others prayed.

At her lowest point she reached out and found that Jesus was still standing with his hand out. Although she felt like she was unworthy of His love she grasped His hand and began to pick herself up. Daily she asked God how He could let this happen to her. God had to know that her children's father was selling drugs, He had to know that her husband didn't really love her, He had to know that her husband would be unfaithful, He had to know that the people in the church and around the church would talk about her and hurt her, and He had to know that she would turn away from His house to go to the streets. How could He know all this and still let it happen? Why her?

Why her? Why you? Why me? We must all come to know that our situation is not final! After every storm the sun shines and a rainbow appears! How do I know this?

> *Now there cried a certain woman of the wives of the sons of the prophet unto Elisha, saying, 'Thy servant my husband is dead; and thou knowest that thy servant did fear the*

> *Lord; and the creditor is come to take unto him my two sons to be bondmen. And Elisha said unto her, 'What shall I do for thee? Tell me what has thou in the house? And she said, Thine handmaid hath not any thing in the house, save a pot of oil. Then he said, Go, borrow thee vessels abroad of all thy neighbors, even empty vessels; borrow not a few: And when thou art come in, thou shalt shut the door upon thee and upon thy sons, and shall pour out into all those vessels, and thou salt set aside that which is full. So she went from him, and shut the door upon her and upon her sons who brought the vessels to her; and she poured out. And it came to pass, when the vessels were full, that she said unto her son, Bring me yet a vessel. And he said unto her, There is not a vessel more. And the oil stayed. Then she come and told the man of God. And he said, Go, sell the oil, and pay the debt, and live thou and thy children of the rest. II Kings 4: 1-7*

This handmaid and her sons were at their lowest point. Her husband dead and the creditors were circling. She was at the point of losing her children. With no one else to turn to she turned to Elisha. I wonder why she had no one else to turn to. We see that she lived in a town with neighbors. Plenty of people lent her empty pots. It's likely that they worshipped together. The scripture notes that her husband did fear the Lord, so we know this was a place where worship wasn't hidden. Surely many people knew her husband he was a son of the prophet. I wonder why those people hadn't given her full pots. Why hadn't they come to her aid? Perhaps because she was now a single mother they distanced themselves from her. Perhaps because she could no longer afford to keep up with the best dressed of the village. Did they look down

on her? Did they talk about her? Did they blame her for the death of her husband? These things we do not know. But we do know that she did not go to the neighbors for help with her circumstances. She unlike many of us turned directly to who she knew could help her, the man of God. We now have the distinct privilege of being able to go directly to the Father ourselves through Jesus Christ.

Why do we not take advantage of our privilege more often? In the previous chapter we learned that God has given each of us some authentic tools, tools designed just for us. What tool did the handmaiden have? All she had was one pot of oil. Could you ever imagine being rich with just one pot of oil? God took what she had combined with her faith in Him and increased her territory. What is in your house? What do you have for God to work with? Oh, trust and believe that you do have something! What you have to offer God is important. Never forget that You are important. All you need do is offer yourself. Jesus continues to stand with his hand out stretched. Grasp hold of His hand and begin to pick yourself up. As you begin to stand continue to seek His face. *He is a rewarded of those who diligently seek him. Hebrews 11:6b.*

What is the reward? Leftovers! Yes leftovers! The handmaiden's pot and those that she borrowed were so many that she had enough to sell and live on. And the oil stayed….it never ran out. My young friend is now living the life of a Sanctified H.O.T.T.I.E. she gave God all she had, at a time when she thought she had nothing to give. She didn't realize, like many of us, her hand is all He wanted. She is now fruitful in everything she puts her

hands to. Her children are in her care, and love God. She is working and being appreciated at her work place constantly. She is active in ministry and happy. Don't ever forget the leftovers, they are running over!

And so why did she or any of us have to endure hard trials and tribulations? It is divine providence. There are things that we must learn in life and learning comes through living. Some H.O.T.T.I.E.s will endure harder trials than others, but each trial is to bring us to the knowledge of Christ. We learn to depend on God for all that we need and that is what He wants from us. Once we really know that all things are from God, He can work with our tools. He can work with us. He has predestined each of our lives and He knows just how much we can take. Just when you think you can't go any lower or take anymore of what the world is throwing your way. He steps in and says remember seasons change. Your situation is not final. And then He asks, "Are you ready to blossom?" The roses don't blossom until the winter frost has melted and saturated the ground in preparation for spring. When it is time for you to blossom, you will be ready for it. Some days may have saturated your ground (heart) with tears, the sorrows from hurt, pain, illness, and/or the death of a loved one. Your ground is ready now, no longer hard. God can plant a seed that will spring up and mature. You are now teachable. You can be shown the mysteries of Him. You can now be trusted with His people. You have been shown how not to treat people, by feeling how others treated you. You have heard what not to say, by hearing what others have said to you. You have been taught to give, while others were

not giving to you. You have learned how to love, while being hated. And as you grasped the hand of Jesus, you regained joy and learned how to smile again, from the inside out. You hearts have been made ready for the Master's use.

Why you? He has need of thee! God wants you! Remember those old Uncle Sam posters used to recruit soldiers? In your mind replace the Uncle Sam with Jesus. He is looking directly at you. His finger pointed directly at you! There is something that you can do for Him that I cannot. It is your authentic tool. Your training and time spent in training has been different from mine. Remember God is equipping you daily.

Do you love God? If you answered yes then your test and trials are the ALL THINGS THAT WORK TOGETHER! Take a look over your shoulder at times when you thought everything was going wrong, you may have thought you were going over a cliff but when you got to the end of the road there was a rainbow. Each twist and turn brought you out safely. Your trial diverted you from a fatal accident. Your test held you just long enough to get you over a broken bridge. And the rainbow at the end was never expected. What you thought would devastate you turned into profit. God is the complete authority of your life. Like the song says, "For the good of them who love the Lord" it works out. I want it to work out for me and YOU! You have a purpose you are of THE CALLED, you are a chosen generation. You are a Sanctified H.O.T.T.I.E.!

"Are you ready to blossom?"

Chapter Six

Be You! Promotion Comes From God!

For promotion cometh neither from the east, nor from the west, nor from the south. But God is the judge: he putteth down one, and setteth up another. Ps 75:6-7

I had a pastor tell me that I should have the attitude of "So what", when it comes to what people say, how people act, what lies people tell, what mess people have my name in and about my past. To tell the truth it offended me! I couldn't believe he would be so callus to think that I could overlook my pain and begin to have that attitude. I was hurting! I did care that people were lying on me, I did care that people had my name in mess, I did care that I had done some things wrong. And it hurt, so how could I have a "So what" attitude? Well, with a little more study, true repentance and a whole lot more prayer, I arrived!

So what! So what! So what, you have made mistakes! Have you repented? Have you learned from your mistakes? Move on!

So what, people still talk about your fall! So what, people still tell the same old story! Same old mess! And they tell the same lies, so what! Move on!

Sanctified H.O.T.T.I.E.

Your baby born out of wedlock is a constant reminder of fornication. The lies you told, still haunt you. The broken friendship still hurts. The scars of your past are your stepping stones for tomorrow. Build a firm fellowship with your tools! Take what you have learned and be you!

Be true to yourself and God and He will keep His promises to you. One can never forget being hurt, or the hurter. A Sanctified H.O.T.T.I.E. learns to repent, and be HOLY, OBEDIENT, TEACHABLE, TRUE, INSPIRING EXCELLENCE. The past is just what it is the past, leave it there. God's mercies are renewed every morning.

> *And, behold, a woman in the city, which was a sinner, when she knew that Jesus sat at meat in the Pharisee's house, brought an alabaster box of ointment, And stood at his feet behind him weeping, and began to wash his feet with tears, and did wipe them with the hairs of her head, and kissed his feet, and anointed them with the ointment. Now when the Pharisee which had bidden him saw it, he spake within himself, saying, This man, if he were a prophet, would have known who and what manner of woman this is that toucheth him: for she is a sinner. And Jesus answering said unto him, Simon, I have somewhat to say unto thee. And he saith, Master, say on. There was a certain creditor which had two debtors: the one owed five hundred pence, and the other fifty. And when they had nothing to pay, he frankly forgave them both. Tell me therefore, which of them will love him most? Simon answered and said, I suppose that he, to whom he forgave most. And he said unto him, Thou hast rightly judged. And he turned to the woman, and said unto Simon, Seest thou this woman? I entered into thine house, thou gavest me*

> *no water for my feet: but she hath washed my feet with tears, and wiped them with the hairs of her head. Thou gavest me no kiss: but this woman since the time I came in hath not ceased to kiss my feet. My head with oil thou didst not anoint: but this woman hath anointed my feet with ointment. Wherefore I say unto thee, Her sins, which are many, are forgiven; for she loved much: but to whom little is forgiven, the same loveth little. And he said unto her, Thy sins are forgiven. And they that sat at meat with him began to say within themselves, Who is this that forgiveth sins also? And he said to the woman, Thy faith hath saved thee; go in peace. Luke 7: 37-50*

What can we learn from this Sanctified H.O.T.T.I.E? Mary of Bethany can teach us all a lesson. Like many of the women chosen for this book, Mary has a reputation and a past. However she did not struggle with either when it came to Jesus and the task at hand.

What boldness! She strolled right into the house where she heard Jesus was eating and began to bless Him. With her past in tow and the current reputation talked about in her presence she did not stop. However she never spoke and remained humble.

Where we as women get hung up is the difference between saying "So what" about our past and facing it with humbled boldness. We most often say "God forgave me and I don't care if they do or not". Well that is not the right spirit. Mary of Bethany was drawn by love. Her love for Jesus, which came from a humble heart, gave her the boldness to do what she did. To stand in front of accusers

and people who thought they were better, she had so much love that those things did not seem to matter.

We some how forget as we approach life with a "So what" attitude that we still need to show love. When we have asked God to forgive us and we begin to move on, don't forget to be humble. Remember often times our lives are on display for all to see. Yes everyone should forgive you when you repent of a sin, but you can not ask everyone to understand or forget. Having an arrogant stance of "So what" can cause more harm than the initial sinful act.

Mary did what God chose for her to do. She kissed, washed and anointed Jesus' feet. With tears of love and humility she boldly accomplished her assignment. Was she hated for this? Was she talked about? No. Actually they questioned Jesus.

Think about how often you ask yourself, why you are talked about when you are only doing what God wants. You get criticized for having a position in the church and you're only doing your job. Have you thought about how much unconditional love you show? Have you examined if you have a spirit of arrogance or humility? Your title does not give you the right to be arrogant. We have all sinned and fallen short of the Glory of God. The way that people respond to you and "your title" is directly related to how much love (true love) you show.

It is extremely hard to change someone's opinion of us, once it has been formed. If you are seen as arrogant, self serving and unloving this will be a tough chapter for you.

You have displayed these characteristics to the world. How do you change them? You must start at ground zero. First you must acknowledge that it is you. It will be hard to influence people that you have or that you are attempting to change. You can not speak empty words or show affection that is not there. As much as we would like to believe that people "don't know". People know!! You are not the only person with the gift of discernment. And let's be real it doesn't take a whole lot of discernment for someone to know when we are being fake.

If you decide tomorrow to ask you sister to forgive you for not speaking to her when she sits right next to you every Sunday, don't pass by her on Wednesday night and not speak. If you have a habit of shutting people out because you are "so focused" on your job, don't ask people to forgive and understand your position and then continue to act like they don't exist. Jesus had the most difficult job, He never shut anyone out. Just as He promoted you, He can demote you. Remember sisters we are to pattern our walk after Him.

Promotion comes from God. He is the one that will be doing your review. Will He be pleased with the Kingdom work you are doing? The work that you do for the church is important, but He will want answers on how you treat His people. If your attitude is driving people away, I'm not sure how much longer you will have your job. You may want to consider a spiritual attitude makeover retreat. Prayer!.

Once you have returned from your spiritual retreat. Whether it was attitude awareness, team building,

management skills, love skills, humility skills, or get rid of arrogance camp, be ready for flesh to meet you at the door. We are striving to be Holy, Obedient, Teachable, True and Inspiring Excellence that is something that the devil does not want. Be prepared for a fight and when you win then you can say "So what!"

Whether you are like me raised as a free hearted girl, boogie boarding and surfing on Huntington Beach. A girl who grew into the knowledge of God and was led to lower the hem on her micro mini skirts. A young lady, woman who turned a wonderful relationship with God into full fellowship with the Father, Son and Holy Ghost, and has been given many gifts of the spirit and is striving to gain them all and excel in them. I am the same woman who God called as a teenager, but had to go through some things before answering that call, from surf board to pulpit. A Sanctified H.O.T.T.I.E. who desires to sky dive, and please God is who I am. While writing this book I have learned more about God and what He desires of me with every chapter. I am grateful for His guidance. I am thankful that He has allowed me to be me, while I operate in His perfect will. So one day if you should look up in the sky and see a pink parachute with the Sanctified H.O.T.T.I.E. logo you will know that I have truly decided to humbly say "So what".

Each morning join me as I say so what to my past and to my present I say……

Be You! Promotion Comes From God!

I am blessed!
I am above and not beneath!
I am beautiful!
I am a lender not a borrower!
I have joy!
I am happy!
I am saved!
I am wonderfully made!
When God made me He made the best!
I will be what God predestined me to be!
If God can take care of the birds of the air,
I know He will take care of me!
Because God made me in the likeness of Him,
there is nobody made better!
I will seek the Lord daily!
I am not of this world!
I am Holy!
I am obedient!
I am teachable!
I am true!
I do inspire excellence!
I am a beautiful woman of God!
I am chosen by God!
Jesus chose me to be His sister!
Jesus died just for me!
If no body loves me God does!
I am elegant!
I am classy!
I am the woman God desires me to be!
I am the woman every man wants!
I am alluring!
I am breath taking!
I am meek!
I am humble!
I love God!
I love the people of God!
I know who I am in God!

Sanctified H.O.T.T.I.E.

I will live with purpose!
I will live a life pleasing to God!
I will possess the promises of God!
I will fulfill my destiny with God's help!

And when I don't feel like praising Him, I will remember "Praise is Non-negotiable"!
And I will bless the Lord at all times, his praise shall continually be in my mouth! Psalm 34:1
I am a Sanctified H.O.T.T.I.E.

"The past is just what it is the past, leave it there. God's mercies are renewed every morning."

Chapter Seven

My Prayer for You

And the very God of peace sanctify you wholly; and I pray God your whole spirit and soul and body be preserved blameless unto the coming of our Lord Jesus Christ. Faithful is he that calleth you, who also will do it .1 Thes. 5: 23-24

I pray that as my sister Sanctified H.O.T.T.I.E., you have found something in the pages of this book that will inspire you to be the best you that you can be. Remember that we are called according to His purpose. God wishes that all would come to the knowledge of Him. Can you spread the word of Jesus Christ? Then you have a ministry. You can reach somebody!

No matter your shape, size or color, you are a Sanctified H.O.T.T.I.E. Do not ever believe that because you don't fit the definition of what society says a "hottie" looks like, being a Sanctified H.O.T.T.I.E. is better! We are the women that God wants to use. We are fit for the master's intentions. A Sanctified H.O.T.T.I.E. is a vessel of honor ready to be an instrument of divine purpose. What society calls a "hottie" is not worthy of the call that I hope you are excepting today.

Father, in the name of your son, Jesus, I adore you! You are an awesome wonder in my life. All praise and honor belong to you. For every sin by commission or omission we

ask your forgiveness. Our past indiscretions please forgive us Lord. I ask a special blessing on the life of the person that has read the pages of this book. God, instill in my sister a desire to be true to you and true to the call that you have placed on her life. Sanctify her wholly; bring peace to her spirit and soul. I ask that you place a burning desire in her heart to continue to walk set apart, sanctified, holy and acceptable to you. Continue to let the Holy Spirit guide and judge her so that she may be presented blameless on the day of your return. Father, bless her household and everything that she sets her hand to do let it be a testimony of your goodness and mercy. May you get the glory at the end of each day. God, I ask that as she continues to walk as a Sanctified H.O.T.T.I.E. that each day she will remember that being a H.O.T.T.I.E. for you means that she will remain holy, obedient, teachable, true and inspire to be excellent. All the praise and honor belongs to you. In Jesus' name I pray, Amen.

My sister take with you this thought, of the women of the bible who touched the heart of Jesus, each one had a past, a present but their future was made perfect in Him. Their lives where changed, however He used what they presented. Don't ever let someone tell you to change before you make a connection with the master. Once you connect with the designer of all things, He will take what you offer and create in you a clean heart and the outer wear He will leave up to the Holy Ghost.

The Holy Ghost will enhance your personality, your class, and your spice and then tailor it for the masters' use. You may find yourself raising your neck line and adjusting your hem line, but it doesn't mean you can't be spicy.

Continue to let the Holy Ghost check you and adapt accordingly, that is what being a Sanctified H.O.T.T.I.E. is about.

When you have made the connection with God and developed a fellowship with the Holy Ghost, Jesus can then add excellence to your walk with Him. Remember we strive to be Holy, Obedient, Teachable, True, and Inspiring Excellence. Excellence is found in Jesus. He is the only one who can present us faultless before the thrown of God.

What's next?

Damita has teamed up with Chef Andre' for her next book, "Stir up the Gift - You Ought to Visit Grandmomma's More Often, A Sanctified H.O.T.T.I.E.'s Guide to Healthy Eating and Living."

For every Sanctified H.O.T.T.I.E. who loves Grandmomma's fried chicken but wants to make it a healthy way, this is the book for you. Chef Andre has taken recipes from grandmothers across the country and enhanced them for healthier eating. Follow the 28 day guide to healthier living and see how much longer you can give God praise on Sunday morning!

While exploring new recipes, Damita infuses biblical principles of gift inheritance. How to sit and receive the oil as it flows to you and preparing the next generation for the gifts you will pass to them.

Damita Jo's motto:

PRAISE IS NON-NEGOTIABLE! *I will bless the Lord at all times, His praise shall continually be in my mouth.*

Psalm 34:1

For more information and to contact Evangelist Carthen www.sanctifiedhottie.net.

About The Author

Determined to see God and to lead others to Him, Evangelist Carthen is a daughter, mother, sister, aunt and friend whose true love for the people of God motivates her to be in continuous study of His word. Studying God's word is her means for knowing what God would have for her and those around her. She believes in going in and possessing the promises of God. Through every mistake, trial and tribulation she understands that true repentance, and determination are key to being the woman that God desires her to be.

Once the owner of Rueben's House, a clean and sober living home for mothers and their children, she finds herself always seeking new ways to help women who have gotten off track. As a Sacramento County Police Chaplain, she saw up-close the brokenness of women, from domestic abuse, drug abuse and death. An executive officer for Angels' Acres Outreach Ministry, she aids in the development of new outreach programs to help underprivileged women and children.

Damita currently resides in Dallas, Texas with her five children. She is a member of Mt. Rose Church; Bishop Jeffery D. Thomas is her Pastor. You can find her often ministering at various Christian Women's events around the country.

She remains grateful to all who have helped shape her Christian walk.

Made in the USA
Charleston, SC
15 July 2013